DESIGNING FEEDBACK

*Performance Measures
for Continuous Improvement*

DESIGNING FEEDBACK

Performance Measures
for Continuous Improvement

CARL G. THOR

CRISP PUBLICATIONS

Editor-in-Chief: *William F. Christopher*

Project Editor: *Kay Keppler*

Editor: *Regina Preciado*

Cover Design: *Kathleen Barcos*

Cover Production: *Russell Leong Design*

Book Design & Production: *London Road Design*

Printer: *Bawden Printing*

Library of Congress Card Catalog Number 97-068252

ISBN 1-56052-468-5

CONTENTS

PART I

PERFORMANCE MEASURES

I.

DEFINING PERFORMANCE

THE TYPICAL DICTIONARY DEFINES performance two ways: "to execute in the proper manner" and "to fulfill a promise or contract."[1] In the performing arts, the execution itself is the contract. But, in the workplace, performance means something else. It deals with how something is (or was) being done. It also focuses on contract fulfillment or result. Something can be done properly but with poor final result. Or, something can be done in an unorthodox manner but still achieve a good result.

Great disputes arise from what is meant by "proper manner" just as major disagreements ensue on whether a promise is "fulfilled" or not. Most people get involved in such arguments frequently in their lifetime. The more alert people learn to pay more attention to defining exactly what is intended before their work starts and to getting feedback on progress from time to time as the work continues.

As working organizations get larger and more complex, individual owners or employees require management systems that help individuals and work groups evaluate the performance of business processes and the adequacy of their results. Thus we have Performance Measurement Systems available for our use.

The Players in Measurement

The person who most needs the information from a Performance Measurement System is the person doing the work (the measuree). Prompt or even real-time feedback to a worker can result in an immediate modification in the manner of working that can lead to better results.

Ironically, in practice, the line worker is often the last person to receive such information. A more senior person in the organization often "owns" and "uses" the measurement system and only selectively gives unsolicited corrective feedback to the measuree.

Measurement specialists (methodologists) assist users of measurement information in formulating the technical definition of the necessary measures. They help develop data-gathering capabilities to support the measures selected.

Whenever a discussion about what is a "good" measure takes place, all three players need to be represented, even in the occasional situation in which one person plays all three roles. The measuree looks for ease of gathering and reporting data, accuracy, and prompt feedback. The user seeks simplicity, such as a sorting or synthesis capability that permits useful interpretation of a complex situation. The methodologist wants assurance that the measure actually reflects what it claims to reflect with accuracy. These different needs often compete with each other in practice.

II.

FORMS OF FEEDBACK

I N BALANCING THE NEEDS of all players, an organization of any size must address feedback issues such as flow and frequency, accuracy and gathering effort, individual and group, and style and format.

Flow and Frequency

Feedback in the form of measured results should go first to the person(s) who can directly use the results to control and improve performance. Information on distribution channel outages should go to the person who controls shipments. Statistical process control information on machine #6 should go to the operator of machine #6. Information on deteriorating corporate image should go to the corporate Public Relations Director. Information on dirt in hotel room #2104 should go to the housekeeper assigned to that room. Of course, others will also be interested later.

The supervisors of all four of the above recipients will eventually need this information, at least in a summarized form. The production scheduler will need to restock after the emergency shipments. Machine #5 might have a similar problem as machine #6. The controller needs to plan for the additional public relations expenditure that may result from image deterioration. The housekeeper needs a longer-handled broom.

Production or service outage information might be generated every day, because corrective action can be applied every day. On the other hand, if the Corporate Image Committee only meets on the third Tuesday of every month, observations might be aggregated and held with only monthly reports. Though small distribution channel outages might be patched daily, aggregated information on which product size is short may only be actionable at the weekly production scheduling meeting where the size mix is adjusted. Thus the summary report might only be weekly to fit the schedule of the weekly production meeting.

At the top of the organization, some measures may only be quarterly or annual. Market share information often arrives on a quarterly basis from outside research survey organizations. Only annual evaluations might be held on such things as employee satisfaction, corporate leadership style, safety program, charitable donations or environmental policy.

Accuracy and Gathering Effort

A philosopher said that it is better to be approximately right than precisely wrong. The extra effort expended to go from approximately right to exactly right is vital in some applications (heart surgery, astronomy) and a waste of time and money in others (civil engineering, catering, cosmetics pricing).

These issues are well illustrated by the data requirements of a complaint-handling group. The "appropriate" level of complaints for a product or service is quite specific to that particular product or service. Whether the level of complaints about a new product is two percent of sales or five percent of sales is nearly useless information in isolation.

However, if very similar products using the same marketing and distribution channels have a complaint level of one percent (or seven percent), we suddenly have useful information. The development of this sort of benchmarking as an active and accessible tool expands an organization's goal-setting capabilities.

When we consider a second time period, we can calculate the level of complaint in comparison to the first period. Now we have the beginning of trend information. Consistency of calculation method, rather than accuracy of the base observation, now becomes critical.

Finally we must address the question of how much information to collect. In complaint handling, the main value is not to know that we are at a bad level of complaints or that our trend is downward. We need to know WHY we receive complaints so we can solve the underlying problems and prevent future complaints. For that we have to gather a great deal of supporting information about the faulty product (raw material lot, production time and line, packaging, distribution lot, type and conditions of use, customer observations). Through Pareto analysis and other techniques that put causes in rank order, we can determine where we have a systematic cause that we can correct.

Individual and Group

"Performance" is sometimes taken to mean how well an individual works. Here it is broader. It can mean any unit of organization, from individuals, to teams, lines, departments, and divisions, to entire organizations. All of these "perform"–or not–as compared to what was intended.

Individuals like to have data about their individual performance, especially if it is "good." This dates from the school report card.

Mature and constructive individuals will accept and learn from data about their "bad" performance, especially if they understand and perhaps have even helped create the basis of evaluation.

In a team environment, where the feedback features team performance, individuals may also be graded on how they perform as a team member. This is a sensitive area, because the judgment (whether made by an outside observer or by the team members themselves) is inherently subjective. Most such evaluation systems work with semi-objective checklists rather than vague feelings, but the evaluation still must be done carefully.

Measuring a team or a department should be limited to what that group can control or importantly influence themselves. They may not be able to control their immediate customers' pleasure with their product or service, but they can control their fidelity to the standard of performance expected from them and their openness to hear about problems from their customers. It is absurd to think that a small work group or production line will consider "high corporate profits" as relevant feedback about THEIR own work.

As the organizational unit gets larger, the measured unit has more under its control, so the scope of the measure becomes broader. The unit can now control things like product or service design, production schedules, complete order cycle time, and availability of proper tools and equipment.

Style and Format

There is an art in giving feedback at any level. Especially at the individual level, how the feedback is given may be more important than its exact content. Not too long ago, feedback was entirely downward, negative and not subject to appeal: *Here is how you do it! If you don't do it this way you're out.* Today, many organizations have evolved to self-managed teams where the team can create the means of working as long as the product or service comes out as planned. Even where "standardized" methods are required, the workforce members may have had a role in creating the methods.

Supervision has become "coaching." Each team member receives positive and negative feedback in the manner that fits his or her personality. Today's supervisors give feedback constructively, emphasizing how the individual or group can improve, rather than how bad things are now. Peers are expected to help their teammates improve rather than waiting for the coach to discover a problem.

Clearly, a corollary of this coaching mentality is that all members of the team understand and perhaps help create the measures used to make the performance judgment. There is no mysterious "intuition" from the coach about whether you will "make it" or not. The focus is on improving work alertness, attention to detail to prevent quality problems, understanding of the customers' needs and an eye to safety and housekeeping. All of these are measured, either by the team itself or by outsider audits, surveys or data gatherings.

Companies often develop visual means of showing group performance at all levels of the organization. These are variously called scorecards, control panels, matrices or metrics. They have been assembled to direct the proper amount of focused attention to the key measures for the group. Kaplan and Norton's balanced scorecard forces attention to four areas (financial, customer, internal processes, and innovation/learning).[2] This breakdown, by including financial, is particularly appropriate at the top of the organization. Similar but more flexible collections of measures have also been labeled "families of measures."[3]

Many short-lead-time operating groups prefer to visualize an airplane control panel where you balance a set of dial positions. Another alternative, the Objectives Matrix, provides a good general format to display the calculation of a performance index in a way that serious observers can understand.[4]

III.

TYPES OF
PERFORMANCE MEASURES

D EFENSE CONTRACTORS IN PARTICULAR are accustomed to cost, schedule and function as the simple imperative to get paid. If the project turns out at or under budget, if it is delivered on time and the product or service "works" as promised, the full payment ensues. This structure can work for a contract-driven organization that delivers a tangible product. But there are organizations with fickle customers and intangible products. And what about the smaller, more intermediary parts of these organizations? All will need some additional terminology to add to the basic cost, time and quality measures.

Profitability

In the private sectors of the world, profitability is why companies conduct business. We measure a company's performance first by profit level and growth. When Wall Street asks which HAVE BEEN the best organizations,

13

the answer is normally provided by profitability data. When the question becomes which WILL BE the best organizations, historical profitability data must be supplemented with data indicating future expectations in the various markets and future intentions of the organizations.

Top managers also realize profit levels and growth do not just happen. They result from a large number of good decisions and well done business process activities. The organizations' managers do not manage profits; they manage processes and make decisions that lead to profits. They need good information on their processes to make the decisions. Thus process excellence is the "driver" of profits, and must be measured in all its aspects. So the key process indicators serve as predictors of future excellence to managers and Wall Street analysts alike.

In fact, some profitability data read alone might be quite misleading. For example, corporate sales growth is made up of the quantity of products/services sold and the price of those products/services. From one period to another, total sales may have grown dramatically (and profit also), but it was driven by major sales price improvements. These were, in turn, permitted by the marketplace because of almost equally strong increases in constituent raw material prices. The actual quantity sold may have started into a serious downturn, which is masked by the strong prices. Only when the price surge winds down will we fully notice the underlying quantity downturn.

Profitability measures in common use include:

- trend in sales, earnings and earnings per share

- level of sales, earnings, and earnings per share
- return on equity, capital or assets
- budget variances
- economic value added

The "physical" data that underlies the financial statement is the main source of the other indicators necessary to provide a balanced analytical picture of an organization.

Productivity and Cost

Productivity

Productivity, the relationship between quantities of output and input of a process, is of major help in understanding an organization. In the example above, productivity analysis would take out the price effects from the sales, raw material, and payroll data and indicate whether the organization is doing a better job of using its resources. It might look at the trend in:

Labor Productivity	Output Quantity/Labor Hours
Material Productivity	Output Quantity/Raw Material Quantity
	Output Quantity/Packaging Material
Energy Productivity	Output Quantity/BTU of Energy Consumed
Capital Productivity	Output Quantity/Inventory Level
	Output Quantity/Assets Employed
	Output Quantity/Capital Inputs
Information Productivity	Output Quantity/Information Cost

Where the output quantity is made up of several different types of product, the numerator could be inflation-adjusted dollars-worth. It is better if the inflation adjustment is specific to each product's price movement rather than some overall product category or whole-economy concept.

You can use an equivalency concept to combine varied outputs. For example, if you have "small" and "large" product variations, the large might be rated as 1.27 "small-equivalents" in regard to labor content, 1.54 small-equivalents in regard to materials, and so on, based on observing standard production procedures. (For most purposes, approximately right will do for equivalencies.)

Where the denominator is stated in dollars, as in information cost or capital, it should be specific-inflation-adjusted. Where it is made up of several physical components, as in materials, they might be combined by inflation-adjusted dollars-worth.

For organizations that have standard costs or an equivalent unit concept, labor and materials productivity can be trended on a ratio of actual usage/standard usage.

The ultimate ratio brings in all the inputs. There are two alternatives:

1. Total Productivity: Output Quantity/All Inputs

Here the inputs are also combined by inflation-adjusted dollars-worth, except that capital employed has to be "annualized" much as if it were all leased.

2. Total Factor Productivity: Value Added/Labor + Capital

Value Added is the output value less inputs that were purchased from outside (normally materials, energy and information). This gives a good measure of what the enterprise added itself: labor, capital and profit. Inflation effects need to be removed where they appear, and the capital needs to be annualized for combination in some form with the labor component.

Figure 1 shows a calculation of each alternative using the same hypothetical data. Both answers are "right." Total Productivity is indifferent whether improvements are made in internal-origin inputs (labor and capital) or purchased inputs (materials, energy and information). A dollar is a dollar! In contrast, Total Factor Productivity gives a leveraged emphasis to the internal-origin inputs. Previously, internal-origin inputs were felt to be more "controllable" than purchased inputs, but that is probably no longer the case. Total Quality Management spends much time on improved purchasing methods and cooperation with suppliers along with energy conservation and information automation. Capital, in contrast, is often controlled tightly by far-off headquarters and labor is increasingly being considered a fixed, or at least semi-fixed, cost.

Because the example provides relative improvements in internal-origin inputs but some slippage in purchased inputs, the Total Factor Productivity improvement is much better than Total Productivity.

17

	Base Year	Current Year
Sales	2.50	2.75
Labor	.80	.85
Materials	1.05	1.16
Energy	.10	.11
Information	.05	.06
Assets Employed	2.00	2.11
Depreciation + Expected Return	16%	16%
Capital Charge	.32	.34

Total Productivity:

% Change

Sales
$$\frac{2.50}{2.32} = 1.078 \qquad \frac{2.75}{2.52} = 1.091 \qquad 1.2\%$$
Labor + Materials + Energy +
Information + Capital

Total Factor Productivity:

Value Added
$$\frac{1.30}{1.12} = 1.161 \qquad \frac{1.42}{1.19} = 1.193 \qquad 2.7\%$$
Labor + Capital

Figure 1. *Total productivity vs total factor productivity example (All data in constant $ million of base year)*

Cost

Unit cost data is essentially upside-down productivity data, input divided by physical output. As above, input costs need to be specific-inflation-adjusted for trend analysis.

Unit Labor Cost	Labor Cost/Units of Product or Service
Unit Variable Cost	Variable Costs/Units
Unit Total Cost	Total Costs/Units

In the public sector, unit cost might often substitute for the lack of a "bottom line." Government outputs often have no assigned price, so the number of units of output is the best available indicator of effort. You can compare this unit cost performance to past unit costs and to the current budget.

The distinction between variable and total costs is important. If the number of units produced is out of the control of the measuree, the total cost comparison may be unfair (unless a flexible budgeting process that adjusts for scale effects is in place). Though total cost may be unfair in terms of controllable past performance, you may use it to look at the immediate future. Low volume activities with a high overhead might be good candidates for outsourcing.

Customer and Marketplace

Customer

Reliable measures of customer satisfaction may be the most important measures for many organizations in that they indicate potential future trouble and often arrive with "surprise" information. The constant problem is that they are time-lagged and are not always "reliable."

Some of the lag is purely mechanical. It takes time for an independent third party to make contact with your customers, get complex information from them, process and interpret the information and get it back to you. But some of the lag is inherent. Field failures or warranty costs do not appear until the product fails. Even direct services experience some lags. Just because a mutual fund customer receives a monthly report eight days after the end of the period doesn't mean he or she will note the error in it immediately.

Companies today pay attention to customer loyalty rather than just customer satisfaction. Will customers make repeat purchases of your product or service? Will they make repeat purchases even in a disadvantageous situation?

For example, until recently, most people were "satisfied" with their long-distance phone service. It usually worked and most people could afford it. But with the breakup of the AT&T monopoly, insurgents such as MCI and Sprint offered the same good service at a lower price. More recently the "tri-opoly" has been challenged by new insurgents such as Excel, offering the same good service at still lower prices. The big three have responded with one-shot cash incentives and/or temporary lower rates to entice customers to change back to them. Here is a stark test of "loyalty." Excel tends to retain its customers because it sells its service through network marketing; customers remain loyal both to Excel and to its representative. Any attempt to measure customer satisfaction through this period is distorted by how recently each customer received a special incentive or a visit from the insurgents' representatives.

In some businesses and in most governments, identification of the customer may be quite difficult. You must satisfy not only the direct user of your product or service, but also any agents between the supplier and user. There may be indirect users beyond the first user: Senator X reads your report and passes it on to Governor Y or staffer Z. There may also be monitors, reviewers or regulators. Books need to satisfy book reviewers or they won't even get to the target customer. Food labels are designed to please the Food and Drug Administration as much as the prototype householder. Even unwilling customers such as prison inmates and taxpayers should still be satisfied by some definition.

Common measures concerning the customer include:

- functional performance of product or service ("quality")

    —on receipt ("moment-of-truth")

    —in the "field"

    —at maintenance time (complaints)

    —on sale or trade-in (value)

- on-time delivery

- mis-shipments, incomplete orders

- order cycle time

- competitive price and product capabilities

21

- image regarding style, new models, innovation
- image regarding helpfulness of service people
- customer retention, active accounts growth
- customer awards

Marketplace

The customer data above comes from the customer by survey or direct contact and from internal records of the company. It reflects the customer's point of view. Data about the marketplace comes from independent third-party measurers and is from the company's point of view.

Companies are interested in overall market share and ranking of their products and breakdowns by product, customer category, distribution channel and region. Some of the breakdowns are more interesting than the overall numbers. Some industries can easily get gross market share by accepting some temporary low-margin business. What is of strategic interest is how they perform in the marketing channels that they have targeted as top priority. Some companies are more interested in position than in level of share. The objective is to rank number one or two in as many businesses as possible, even if number one only carries an eight percent market share, rather than being number four in a market, but with 19 percent.

Companies need to track new product data also. What percent of the business is from "new" products or "high tech" products or some other cross-cutting category? What is the new product development cycle time?

Process Quality

Customer and marketplace measures deal with what might be called "external quality": the quality of a product or service as viewed by the external customer. "Internal quality" leads to external quality. The business processes of the organization have to run smoothly, and whenever a problem occurs, the company learns from it and improves methods to prevent it from reappearing. If the processes are well designed and the employees understand and follow the collection of good practices that make up the processes, external quality problems should not appear. The product or service "works," is on time and carries no unnecessary cost burden.

The key concept in process quality is waste. In a broad sense, the search for and elimination of waste are the measures of process quality. In a manufacturing setting, Shigeo Shingo identifies seven types of waste:[5]

- defects
- overproduction
- waiting time
- transport time
- processing waste
- excess inventory
- excess motion

Standard accounting methods only capture two of these, defects and processing waste. Overproduction at the individual machine level, when relabeled "economies of scale," may appear to avoid another waste: the underutilization of expensive equipment. Excess inventory creates an "asset" on the books, which provides a misleading sense of security.

Only when we view the production system as a whole do we see that these wastes are a source of the low-quality, high-cost and long-response-time products that were becoming standard in the United States in the 1970s and 1980s. The just-in-time system pioneered by Toyota and now carried on by many leaders in North America shows the critical role the supposedly "mature" factory flow processes play in an organization's success.

The Shingo Prize for Manufacturing Excellence has been awarded in North America since 1988 to promote the orientation toward waste elimination in this broader sense. The accounting implications of this approach are found in "Management Accounting in Support of Manufacturing Excellence," a study of Shingo Prize recipients sponsored by the IMA Foundation for Applied Research.[6]

Waste in service industries and government is more subtle but differs little from Shingo's manufacturing wastes. Most notorious is wasted time, but in many cases the original time expectation and "production specifications" are not as clear or even do not exist. Some service organizations, such as hotels and restaurants, have successfully implemented customer-oriented just-in-time service. The backrooms of banks and insurance companies have progressed toward reducing cycle times using "cells," a common manufacturing process.

Most of the process quality measures in common use are physical measures, but one common measure involves dollar aggregations: the Cost of (Poor) Quality. This measure calculates what the organization's total cost would be if everything were done perfectly the first time and compares that number to actual current cost.

This means that many types of costs would not be incurred. Internal nonconformance cost such as scrap, rework, and downtime would disappear. External costs such as warranty cost, complaint handling, returns, sales errors and quality-related concessions would vanish. And, more controversially, common prevention activities such as quality training, vendor certification, inspection, and reviews could be at least partially disbanded. All of these expenses add up to an often shocking percentage of total cost, perhaps 25 to 30 percent. See Figure 2 for a sample calculation. Cost of (Poor) Quality can provide a wake-up call to a senior management that does not grasp the central importance of having a quality orientation.

Cost of (Poor) Quality measures the big picture, but for analytical purposes we must break it down to actionable specific measures. Common process quality measures are:

- error rates (errors per million opportunities for error)

- scrap and rework

- unplanned machine downtime, emergency maintenance

- first-pass yield

AMALGAMATED ZOT INDUSTRIES

Amalgamated's Cost Data:

Corporate sales:	$6,000,000/year
Units sold:	60,000/year
Average selling price:	$100/zot
Cost of goods shipped:	$80/zot
Average profit margin:	$20/zot
Units produced:	62,400/year
Labor cost:	$24/zot
Average rework cost:	$12/reworked zot
Standard customer freight:	$2/zot
Money cost:	15%/year
Employee hours:	2,000/year
Benefit multiplier:	$1.40 \times$ base wage

Calculation of Cost of (Poor) Quality:

1. Returns

8% of the products shipped are returned; of these, half are scrapped and half are reworked and reshipped. Return freight is $3/zot.

2,400 units scrap $\times$ $80 cgs	=	$192,000
4,800 return freight $\times$ $3		14,400
2,400 additional rework $\times$ $12		28,800
2,400 back-to-customer freight $\times$ $2		4,800

2. Inspection

There are six inspectors (wage: $15/hour) and one quality training specialist ($30,000/yr).

7 employees $\times$ $30,000 $\times$ 1.40	=	$294,000

3. Production Scrap and Rework

There is a 3% scrap rate on zot wire. It is purchased at $2,100 per spool from World Wide Wire Works and 1,000 spools enter the plant per year. Scrap is sold to a hanger-maker at 1/3 of the original price. Production rework takes up 15% of production labor's time.

$2,100,000 wire $\times$ .03 $\times$ 2/3	=	$ 42,000
60,000 $\times$ $24 $\times$ .15 production rework		216,000

Figure 2. Cost of (poor) quality

4. Work-In-Process Inventory

The industry averages 20 turns of WIP. Amalgamated achieves only 12 turns.

$$\frac{62{,}400 \times \$80}{\text{WIPi}} = 20 \text{ (industry)}$$

WIPi = 249,600

$$\frac{62{,}400 \times \$80}{\text{WIPa}} = 12 \text{ (Amalgamated)}$$

WIPa = 416,000

Excess inventory: $166,400 × .15   = $ 24,960

5. Maintenance

The six-person maintenance department spends 30% of its time on unplanned crisis maintenance. Wage for maintenance workers is $17/hour. The industry standard for machine downtime is 20%. Amalgamated is down 30% of the time. The machines are on the books at $4,000,000.

6 × $34,000 × 1.4 × .3 crisis	=	$ 85,680
$4,000,000 × (.3 − .2) × .15	=	60,000

6. Sales and Customer

Half the product returns require one day of salesman crisis time each to keep the customer. Average order is $800. Salesmen are paid $40,000 salary. 20% of the salesman crisis calls fail, each failure resulting in a loss of $20,000/year of sales.

$240,000/800 = 300 crisis visit days ×		
($40,000 × 1.4/250 available days)	=	$ 67,200
60 calls fail × $20,000 × .2 margin	=	240,000

Grand Total, #1–#6 Costs of (Poor) Quality   **$1,269,840**
% of $6,000,000 Sales   **21.2%**

Figure 2.   Cost of (poor) quality (continued)

- process cycle time

- work-in-process inventory turns

- supplier performance and profile

- benchmarking activity level

- process capability

- capacity utilization

- changeover experience

- level of automation

- score on quality assessment

- documentation accuracy and timeliness

Workforce

The workforce is measured directly in labor productivity and indirectly in various customer satisfaction and process quality measures. But other measures that focus on the workforce itself rather than on its product or service should also be part of any measurement system.

Safety and Housekeeping

Every manufacturing plant and many manufacturing-like services (utilities, transportation) should have measures of safety. The most common measure in the United States is "OSHA Reportables" per 200,000 work hours, which is required to be reported to OSHA (Office of

Safety and Health Administration) periodically. A reportable is essentially any occurrence requiring more than routine first-aid or that results in lost worktime.

Because Total Quality Management tries to deal with prevention more than correction, some prefer a measure of unsafe acts per work-hour, regardless of the actual consequences of those acts. This data is difficult to gather, because it is subjective. A few financially oriented companies still measure only lost time and workers' compensation costs on the grounds that only these have incurred an actual cost to the company.

"Clean-Room Industries" like semiconductor manufacturing will also measure temperature, pressure, and particulate matter out-of-control occurrences, due to the critical nature of their production processes.

Many organizations measure housekeeping through audit-based assessments against a predetermined set of criteria. The resulting score may be a number of points out of 100 maximum. Some organized visual control programs are measured in stages, such as this example from Boeing:

Stage 1.   Status Quo
Stage 2.   Visible Evidence of Change, Eliminating the Bad
Stage 3.   Visible Evidence of Change, Bringing in the Good
Stage 4.   Reliable Methods in Place
Stage 5.   Self-Sustaining Good Practice

Verbal descriptions that can be used as calibration references accompany each stage.

Training

Most organizations measure the amount of training given to their employees, usually by employee category. The most commonly used measures compare training hours to total hours of scheduled work and training cost as a percent of payroll. The former is a pure measure of quantity where "up is good." The latter combines quantity and price. It will go up with an increase in the physical amount of training, but it will also go up as the training becomes more extravagant.

More sophisticated organizations attempt to measure the quality of training as well as the quantity. It is easy to state the quality measure: proven competence in the subject of the training. But proof of competence is only clear regarding some operating-floor technical training and computer software applications. It is quite unclear in most management training.

Another training-related measure is meeting employee skill-mix targets, such as percent of employees who can use a certain software program or repair a certain machine. The author developed a skill-mix measure called the Kiwanis Club Measure for an issue-oriented nonprofit organization. It was simply what percentage of the organization's staff could give a 15-minute speech to a Kiwanis Club on the organization's key issue with one day's notice.

Closely related are measures of job rotation capability and practice. A quality organization will cross-train many people to do jobs other than their own, both for vacation relief and individual development and job interest. The organization should not just shift people in an emergency but should make it a routine practice, enough to keep up everyone's alternate skills.

Other Workforce Measures

Other workforce measures might include:

- workforce satisfaction surveys
- employee turnover and absenteeism
- suggestions submitted
- wellness and health experience
- computer capability and connectivity
- level of decision-making

Community

Finally, consider measures relating to the organization's relationship with the broader community. These include:

- environmental initiatives and results
- educational partnering
- employee community leadership
- benchmarking receptivity
- public image assessment

Part II

How Measures Are Used

IV.

STRATEGIES, GOAL-SETTING AND FOCUS

W E HAVE SAID THAT MEASURED RESULTS provide feedback that allows employees to manage and improve business processes, provided the measured results go to the "right" person in a timely and consistent manner. There is another proviso: the measure must provide feedback on the right issue(s). Chapter I includes a long list of types of performance measures, but which are the right measures in a particular situation?

Unfortunately, we have no universal answer. If it is true that you get what you measure, then you should measure what you want to get! Profit-seeking organizations want profit, but the current route to profit varies from organization to organization. In some places, product or service quality improvement is the chosen route. In others, cost-reduction is the answer. Still others emphasize new products or quicker customer response. Nonprofit or public-sector organizations may emphasize becoming closely connected to a popular policy or issue, but also with some budget performance qualifying goal. Unfortunately, the most common answer is a variation on: all of the above, no particular focus, whatever it takes. Before measurement can be of much value, an organization needs a strategic focus.

If an organization is organized at all, the place to get help in the issue of "what they want to get" is a strategic plan or its informal equivalent.

Planning a Strategy

Having a strategic plan is important, but having planned the organization's strategy is more important. It isn't the plan; it's the planning! A start-up organization usually has one grand strategy that is the basis for its creation. As long as that strategy keeps everyone's attention and provides the expected success, nothing much needs to change. But over time, when great success or even some disappointment occurs, the questions come out: What else do we do? What do we do next? What are our priorities?

A good strategic planning exercise gives each alternative a hearing. Analyze and objectively criticize each option's implications for the whole organization over time. You usually discover that all the great ideas cannot be implemented due to constraints such as capital or workforce shortages. Thus, ideas get combined, modified, postponed or accelerated by mutual agreement.

Strategic planning involves an interrelationship among the top, middle and bottom of an organization. Some companies debate whether top-down or bottom-up planning is better, but these two extremes are both rare and ineffective. The usual practice looks more like a tennis match, with senior management proposing a few key guidelines, the full organization answering with some tentative ideas, senior management reacting and expanding, middle management revising, and so on. In fact, two Japanese authors have now proposed a "middle-outward" organization style that better states what really happens.[7]

Surprisingly large variations appear when we look at how different organizations approach strategic planning. Some of the variations come from terminology problems, but others arise out of organizational personality or what the authors of *Built to Last* call the "successful habits of visionary companies."[8]

Here is a consensus strategic planning sequence:

Step 1.
Vision/Mission/Values

The vision is a hoped-for snapshot of the organization in, say, ten years. What matters most to the organization? What is its key purpose and direction? It often reflects how the key customers or general public might be expected to view the organization, with words like "leading source of . . . ," "most respected . . . ," or "synonymous with . . ." The clearest of all are Henry Ford's vision of "producing a car that everyone can buy" and NASA's "put a man on the moon by the end of the decade."

The vision's time frame is the future looking back toward the present. The mission is current focus looking outward. What is the central thing the organization is now doing or trying to do? A clear mission statement should reflect both the main customer-oriented thrusts and the dominant improvement programs. An organization might be "modifying the operating organization to provide improved customer response time." It might be "developing new computerized services to help customers solve more complex problems." Or "integrating the two recent acquisitions to provide uniformly excellent service." Three years from now the company may need a new mission statement, but the vision and values should rarely change.

Most organizations have implicit values that you can infer from statements or actions of previous leadership, but it is now common to try to make these values explicit. This becomes more necessary as organizations become global or otherwise diverse, and you can no longer rely (if you ever could) on similarity of cultural background to ensure that all employees will react to a challenge in the same way. Issues covered may include responsibility to customers, employee development, access to information, obedience to laws and environmental responsibility.

Step 2.
Customer Identification and Needs

Once strategic planning becomes routine, customer identification gets routine also. But even then, new products/services may broaden the list. The first strategic plan often has trouble recognizing the various levels of direct and indirect customers. This is especially true in the public sector, but even "standard" private-sector products often have multiple levels of distributors and indirect users downstream from the obvious customers.

The customer's needs may be quite profound. Sometimes a progressive supplier recognizes a customer's emerging need before the customer does. Boeing focuses on the "enduring needs" of its customers, potentially in partial opposition to what the customer emphasized last month. A product with a long life cycle requires a long-term view of customer service.

Step 3.
Environmental Scan and Organization Resources

Each plan requires a new and objective look at the current and projected future environment. Critical issues include:

- regional, national and world economic outlook

- current trends in markets, both the key products/services of the organization and the markets of its leading industrial customers and suppliers

- political and regulatory developments

- availability of needed resources (manpower, capital, materials, energy, information)

- changes in management practices and investor expectations

- competitor activities and trends

It is also wise to include a review of what Boeing calls the "enabling qualities and capabilities" of the organization. A good business climate is not enough.

The organization must have in place or "on order" the requirements for doing business in the current and projected future business climate.

Step 4.
Core Processes and Projects

What is the organization now doing that needs to continue? What else needs to be started or strengthened to fit with vision, mission and values statements? What are the relative priorities and timings of these activities? Where is the focus to be? What will the company NOT do in the time frame of the plan?

Step 5.
Goal-Setting

Set goals at different times in the planning process with the appropriate degrees of specificity. Figure 3 shows one cascading set of goal statements. The vision statement might even include a goal. Henry Ford wanted "everyone" to be able to buy his car.

Goals for core processes and projects will often be aggregated or general, using words like "substantial" or perhaps even "company-wide savings of $10 million." The second statement is measurable at the company level, but it alone gives no useful guidance to a division manager or process owner. Supplement these early and general goals with specific objectives later in the planning process.

Level 1:   Dominate the frunk market

Level 2:   Increase our share of the rigid frunk market and obtain major adoptions of flexible frunks

Level 3:   Increase rigid frunk market share to 26% and obtain five or more major adoptions of flexible frunks by the end of next year

Level 4:   By the end of next year: (a) increase rigid frunk market share to 26% (without accepting any business below 32 cents operating contribution and limiting advertising to last year's actual) and (b) obtain at least five flexible frunk adoptions (worth $5 million annual value, using no more than guideline promotional allowances)

Figure 3.   Cascading goals

Step 6.
Detailed Plan and Measures

At this point, a detailed plan can be developed from the agreed-upon process and project priorities. It will be hard to reconcile intended activity with resource constraints, and several drafts and discussions are usually required. Every middle-manager advocate of a certain direction will want more resources and more project time with less immediately deliverable results than is required to make the plan "balance." But everyone will eventually put some additional stretch into their project budgets and drop some other minor things they are doing to create appropriate focus.

The best time to develop the required measures is when a pet project is approved for inclusion in the strategic plan. Some of the measures are obvious: resources used, time of delivery and project financial result were already part of the plan itself. But you will also need to measure the more subtle aspects, such as effects on customers or suppliers, documentation needs, safety considerations, rework and error rates.

Step 7.
Communication and Roll-Out

After you have balanced the strategic plan and defined the scope and general resources required for each project or process, you can create the detailed execution plans. These plans add the "who" and "how" to the existing "what" and "when." The plans are made known to employees through various means of communication. The traditional downward directive has been replaced by various means of mutual agreement.

The Japanese developed an extension of strategic planning called Hoshin Planning. It begins where traditional strategic planning begins but doesn't end until every employee knows and accepts his or her own role in making the plan work. Texas Instruments created a similar process called "Catchball," in which each employee questions and then finally signs off (after modification, in some cases) on his or her responsibilities for each deliverable.

Perhaps it is now clear why a little book on "performance measurement" spends so much time on strategic planning. Most consulting projects originally called "measurement" turn out to be at least partly about lack of clarity in the organization's strategic intent. Many high-level goals turn out to distort later measurement activity.

It is widely assumed that measurement is something technical specialists can do without regard to the "big" issues of top management. Not true! If you get what you measure, those who develop the measures must know exactly what the organization wants to get. When a plan roll-out collects action plans and promises, it must simultaneously develop how those action results will be measured.

V.

ORGANIZATIONAL ALIGNMENT

A N ANNUAL STRATEGIC PLAN provides an important alignment vehicle in a far-flung organization.
Between plans, however, the organization depends
on its performance measurement system to keep order and
to alert everyone to unexpected problems or exceptions.
Other forms of alignment include management training
and rituals, recognition practices, and the company maga-
zine or e-mail system. But the performance measurement
system should be in front of everyone every day.

Vertical Alignment

Vertical alignment refers to consistency and coordination
between performance measures of the same category (e.g.,
productivity, quality or customer satisfaction) as expressed
at different organizational levels. Consistency is not the
same as identity. Occasionally a measure can be aggregated upward throughout all or most of the organization
without adjustment, but that is the exception rather than
the rule.

Financial reporting provides most of the examples of measures that you can use everywhere. Sales revenue is usually combinable from wherever it occurs. So are operating cost and payroll. Value-added can apply to any size or level of operating unit. With some clear definitions, "errors" per million "opportunities for error" can be aggregated across disparate organizations. In safety, OSHA reportables can be aggregated. But just because these can be and are combined doesn't mean they are easy to interpret. A surge in OSHA reportables per 200,000 hours means something quite different in a corporate office than it does in an explosives plant.

In most cases, you can best serve the cause of rapid and effective improvement (the main reason we measure) by letting each part of the organization have the measures they need most in their own area. Corporate strategic thrusts should still be represented. The appropriate compromise is to declare that every part of the organization should measure some aspect of each key thrust, but the detail is left to them. Figure 4 illustrates the situation.

In this example, we have three "families of measures" from three different levels of the same organization. The corporation has decided to emphasize four strategic thrusts: productivity, quality, customer satisfaction and workforce excellence. Thus each component part of the organization, including the corporate executives themselves, will develop a family of measures that reflects the four thrusts. The family of measures will also provide the departments with all the key measures they need to run their part of the business. They may include "wild card"

Category	Corporate	Plant	Regional Sales Office
Productivity	Inflation-adjusted value added/ employee	Weighted units/ work hour	Weighted contacts/ salesperson
Quality	Award score	Rework	Order cycle time
Customer	Survey score	On-time delivery	% of customers "active"
Workforce	Training/employee	OSHA reportables/ 200K hours	$ of salespersons "certified"
Wild cards	% of business deregulated	WIP turns	Customer awards
	Public image survey	Environment index	Complaint resolution

Figure 4. Vertically aligned families of measures

measures in addition to those linked to the strategic thrusts.

In each category, the respective levels of the organization reflect on what, at their levels, would represent productivity, quality, customer satisfaction and workforce excellence. Then each notes what is missing to make the family complete, and these missing measures enter through the wild card slot(s). They can choose other measures from the thrust categories or measures from other categories as appropriate. Nothing prevents these groups from developing and using other measures "off-line," but the official family of measures is created to provide focus to the organization. Everyone should concentrate on these measures first.

47

Horizontal Alignment

Horizontal alignment is coordination and understanding of the measures for each organizational level across all parts of the organization. This means that all the regional sales offices in the example above might measure all or most of the same things by order of the National Sales Manager. Or they consciously might not due to clearly recognized differences.

In pharmaceutical sales, for example, salespeople make contacts with doctors. Orders may result later, but the connection between contacts and sales is unclear and lagged. In used car sales, in contrast, it is direct sales dollars that count. A nonsale "contact" is a waste of time. In a hypothetical conglomerate that had pharmaceutical sales regions and used car sales regions, the latter would probably choose to measure sales per salesperson rather than weighted contacts per salesperson. The concept of used car salesperson "certification" would be very different as would "order cycle time."

Other common horizontal alignment thrusts include consistent measurement of safety, maintenance, and inventory turns across plants; training hours and course effectiveness across divisions; computer connectivity and applications across locations; and employee skill mix. These are usually a primary concern of a corporate staff coordinator, who needs consistency to coordinate organization-wide initiatives.

Horizontal alignment presents a greater challenge when an organization becomes multinational or even global. Rationales surface from lower in the organization about why worldwide consistency is neither possible nor desirable. Some of these arguments may be valid, but the corporate coordinator needs to understand the exceptions and explain them whenever worldwide comparisons are made.

Back in the 1970s, IBM had a Common Staffing System that allowed them to compare and understand staff groups across international boundaries.[9]

Balance Among Measures

An organization aligns itself in part through the families of measures used at each level in response to vertical strategic thrusts and horizontal staff-driven consistency requirements. Simply choosing the measures isn't the entire task. Much thought needs to go into the relative importance of each of the measures within each family of measures.

The discussion about the appropriate number of performance measures goes back at least as far as the God-Moses meeting that produced the Ten Commandments. The normal focused family of measures has four to six components, either single measures or subindexes. The term has been applied to as many as 12 to 15 components, but this is not focus in its usual meaning. Requiring that everyone remember the family of measures' components will help keep the number down!

Each component receives a weight. All the weights add up to 100. The prime criterion for the weight is what do you want employees to concentrate on during the time period.

Sometimes a hard-to-measure idea can be captured better in a multi-measure index than in a single measure. You may have four or five important quality measures or six or seven important customer measures, but the top-of-organization group only has room for one of that category. In this case, construct a quality index or a customer index and enter only the index result into the final family of measures.

Company Environmental Index	Weight	Performance	Result
Regulatory violations (severity weighted)	.30	104	31.2
Internal program milestone attainment	.25	90	22.5
Waste release progress (subindex of air, water, solid)	.20	115	23.0
Environmental program cost (net of program savings)	.10	85	8.5
Community opinion survey results	.15	106	15.9
Total	1.00		101.1

Corporate Family of Measures	Weight	Performance	Result
Inflation-adjusted value added/employee	.20	105.2	21.0
Customer index	.30	93.0	27.9
WIP inventory turns	.10	110.0	11.0
Cost of (poor) quality/sales	.25	95.7	23.9
Environmental index	.15	101.1	15.2
Total	1.00		99.0

Figure 5.   Environmental index in a corporate family of measures

The same has been done with "involvement" and "ethics," where the subindex components are only rough surrogates for the measured idea. Figure 5 presents an example of an Environmental Index that mixes together internal efforts, external results and external attitudes.[10]

The company performed well in terms of external environmental results and perception thereof, but they lagged behind plan in the internal projects and cost savings. This result can be the entire family of measures for the Environmental Manager and can also be plugged into the corporate level family of measures in Figure 5.

Though three of the five corporate measures improved for the period, including the Environmental Index, the two weightiest factors (customer satisfaction and cost of quality) were down for the period, causing the entire family to show up as a negative 1.0 percent (99.0).

Four to six components for a family of measures is a good number. Any more and people can't focus on all of them, and any less may not achieve the results you want. The weights should be between ten and 35 percent. Less than ten percent tends to cause people to ignore that component. More than 35 percent causes almost exclusive attention to that measure, defeating the "balance" policy.

VI.

OUTPUTS AND OUTCOMES

E VEN AFTER YOU HAVE ESTABLISHED and weighted
your measures and checked the results, you do
not have a complete picture. You are still missing
an element that becomes especially visible in the public
sector and in research. You know whether a particular output is free of error and satisfies the immediate customer,
but sometimes it takes time to judge whether the product
is truly of value. This toothpaste appears to do the job,
but only at the next trip to the dentist will you discover
whether it prevented cavities. Our research program has
identified many possible causes of *phrogetania symbosis,* but it
will be years before we know if we have an effective cure.

It is even more difficult to judge effectiveness in the
public sector. You can measure a government position
paper as finished (productivity), well-written (quality), and
interesting (customer satisfaction), but will it convert any
editorial writers or congresspeople and lead to reform in
its area? Now we are talking about "outcomes" instead
of outputs.

Outcomes are generally severely time-lagged and
sometimes unclear but of great importance. We can

measure diplomas granted, but we really want educated and employable citizens. We can measure inoculations and disease-prevention pamphlets, but we want eradicated diseases. We can count water pollution interventions, but we want appropriate fish populations. The relationship of outcome to other productivity terms is shown in Figure 6.

So families of measures should consider including both output and outcome oriented measures. We need a practical compromise between the need to run the business now and the need to make policy or research results happen well in the future. Any outcome measures now

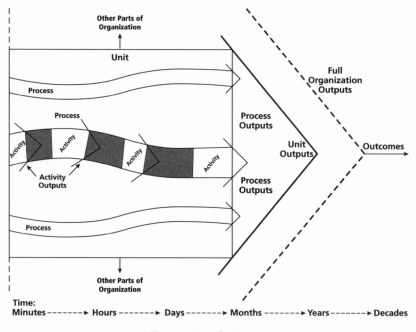

Figure 6.   Outcomes

available may reflect work performed long ago. Perhaps you can set intermediate "milestone" measures to reflect progress towards a future outcome.

In addition to working outward from today's outputs, which is typically done in strategic planning exercises, outcomes need to be "worked backwards" to discover what you need to do today to enable those future outcomes. Hopefully some of today's outputs are the right ones. But you may identify some missing outputs through this process, which resembles Quality Function Deployment.[11]

VII.

PREDICTIVE MEASURES

P REDICTIVE MEASURES ARE THOSE in which changes in a measure's results forecast or predict changes in another measure's results. These are common in national macroeconomics, where housing starts predict certain industrial activities or where weather predicts commodity prices. But there are now substantial attempts to apply this thinking at the firm level.[12] Some of the pairs of predictive measures in use are "common sense" relationships where statistical proof is hardly necessary, but other less obvious pairs have been subjected to heavy statistical testing.

Most of the best work has been done in predicting customer behavior. Customer satisfaction is related to many marketing and financial variables such as sales, customer retention, operating costs and public image. How do you achieve customer satisfaction? One suggestion is through employee satisfaction. Satisfied and well-oriented employees will do a better job of working with their customers than "average" employees.

One financial services firm is working on a chain where field management strength leads to better agent recruiting which in turn leads to higher sales and profits. With this in mind, the company has renewed its emphasis on field management training and support.

In the factory, forecast accuracy leads to smoother schedules and thus higher labor productivity. Successful attainment of shorter cycle time predicts lower operating cost and thus lower product costs. Electronic applications can reduce time and error rates.

In selecting appropriate focus measures for a family of measures, give special attention to the more basic measures that themselves are predictors of other key measures later in the production cycle.

PART III

GETTING IMPROVEMENT THROUGH MEASURES

VIII.

PERFORMANCE MEASURES ARE NOT ENOUGH

A N ORGANIZATION CAN CREATE a set of performance measures that meets all the criteria discussed above (strategy linkage, alignment, balance) and still be ineffective as an operating organization and even "information poor." One cause of this could be poor communication of the measured results, either through infrequent usage or complex methodology. Problems like that can be noted and corrected. The most subtle and pernicious problem occurs where the management culture and style do not respect the value of a comprehensive measurement system, and executives, often unintentionally, undermine the system that has been put in place.

Leadership and the Driver Concept

One principle of this approach to performance measurement is that measured results should go first to the person in the organization with the most direct responsibility for that variable so that he or she can make timely corrections and improvements. Of course, this assumes that the responsible local leader is empowered to actually make those changes. If only the top leader of the organization can approve changes, however small, the whole alignment issue becomes moot. Then the organization has only one "user" of the information.

So this approach requires delegation and trust in the capabilities of subordinates. Resolve any doubts along these lines through additional training or better tools, or replacement of the subordinate before problems arise.

Another principle is that lower-level physical information in an empowered organization leads to higher-level financial results. This requires trust in the data as well as in the employees generating and interpreting it. This is most challenging when customer-origin data reveal a finding that is counter to what has been previously assumed. The organizational leader then has a tough call. Many times the customer is "more right" than the experts inside the supplying organization. But sometimes a bold leader can see a step beyond ordinary customers and make a decision that satisfies the customers even more than they thought they could be satisfied. That explains why bold leaders make large salaries (and have a high turnover rate).

A similar problem occurs when a bold leader "sees beyond" the organization's latest strategic plan or continuous improvement initiatives and orders an unexpected "breakthrough" strategy shift. Though this wreaks havoc with carefully crafted measurement and communication tactics and confuses diligent employees, the measurement system is the servant of the organization leaders' latest intentions. Balance forms the basis of a good performance measurement system, but if the company calls for a "crusade," the measurement system must be able to adapt quickly.

A good measurement system in any style of organization is transparent. Many people have the information to mount prompt and effective challenges to doubtful ideas. Thus the label "subversive" has sometimes been (properly) attached to measurement systems by opponents. But this is a good form of subversion, because a quick challenge and resolution of an issue is much better for the long-term health of the organization than secrecy, delay, lingering doubts and lack of focus.

IX.

COMMUNICATION OF RESULTS

G OOD COMMUNICATION OF MEASURED results allows leadership to be exercised at all levels of the organization. An organization cannot claim to be data-driven if the data, information and knowledge that result cannot be understood and applied by the responsible person.

Style

Communication style should fit with leadership style and strategic intent. An organization that emphasizes empowerment and preventive action by everyone in the organization needs to ensure that all employees receive the information they need to act correctly. This requires a thoughtful and complex communication strategy, because different people receive information in different ways. An organization that takes pride in its central direction and predictability needs only to ensure that all the data makes it to the top of the organization and that comfortable generalities get communicated downward and outward.

A recent study of corporate measurement practices among well-known companies asked participants which of the following five styles best describes his or her organization:[13]

(1)   strictly "need to know"

(2)   periodic structured downward

(3)   "open-door," informal

(4)   frequent, multi-means, up and down, some information withheld

(5)   frequent, multi-means, up and down, nothing withheld

About half the respondents answered (4) as expected, but there were some responses in each of the other categories. Though (4) and (5) seem progressive and modern, they do not ensure effective communication of measured results. Organizations can be virtually paralyzed by too much information.

One medium-sized financial organization has 47 "key" measures that float up to the top leader in a dense, tabular report. The top leader, a brilliant "quick-study," scans the information for new issues and then puts it away. The rest of the organization, seeing little visible evidence of the use of those measures, brands them as useless and concentrates instead on "their own" measures in their responsibility areas. There is no common ground for discussion, until the financial results come in each quarter (taking everyone by surprise).

In contrast, (1) and (2) seem tight and secretive. But a careful (and possibly even participative) selection of what measures are needed by whom can sometimes be effective.

Means

There is an extremely wide variation in what means are used to communicate measured results and how effective they each are in reaching the employees. The only common ground that the successful organizations share is that they have experimented a great deal with various approaches before they arrived at current practice.

Cartoonists enjoy the idea that a company bulletin board is the only place you can ensure something will NOT be read! But the best of the empowered organizations proudly display all kinds of complex information on bulletin boards as a major part of their approach. A major difference is that these bulletin boards are "owned" by a specific, usually small, group. They contain a combination of instructions, schedules and results that are "must reading" for that group. Which came first, the bulletin board or the attitude that an empowered employee needs information to succeed? It does not matter as long as it works.

Many of these boards are "white boards" rather than cork-like bulletin boards (with glass covers and locks). This is not a trivial difference. White boards depend on "original" writing and graphing by the covered group. Cork boards have traditionally received pre-prepared paper from authority figures armed with thumbtacks or pins. Which better symbolizes empowerment?

Modern companies also convey important results information by e-mail, videos, and special meetings in addition to (or even as substitute for) company publications and quick mention at routine meetings. All of these means can bear a more detailed message. In this age of "sound bites" and "sound bytes," it is gratifying that empowered employees care enough about the message to require some level of detail. Obviously if the "findings" from measured results commonly get translated to corrective action, the employees will pay more attention to the results.

In some situations, especially on the factory floor, the appearance of smoothly flowing operations is reasonable current evidence of effective operations. In just-in-time organizations, the signaling system is explicitly designed to pay exaggerated attention to non-smooth flow, so absence of uproar is good news! However, this does not argue for less measurement. We may not need an indicator of smooth operations, but we do need to know how "un-smooth" an interrupted or poorly functioning operation is in order to formulate corrective and preventive action.

X.

FORMAT AND GRAPHICS

SUCCESSFUL COMMUNICATION IS NOT just a matter of having enough messages in the right place. The target audience needs to understand and remember the information they have received. The challenge is to simplify the information without altering the way it is interpreted. Some newspapers are notorious for oversimplified or actually dishonest graphical presentations, and where public newspapers go you can assume corporate communicators and their captive executives will follow.

Visual Workplace

The movement toward localized "white boards" in the workplace is part of a larger movement toward simplification and visual control in many parts of an organization. The Japanese-origin 5S approach encourages the individual worker to take more interest in organizing the local workplace. Five Japanese words starting with "S" translate into English as: Sort, Standardize, Shine, Sustain and Straighten.[14] The underlying message is another way of getting to empowerment; your surroundings influence the discipline with which you work.

Part of 5S and other similar housekeeping drives is to find an "official" place for every item in the workplace and an "official" use for every unit of space. Color-coding and

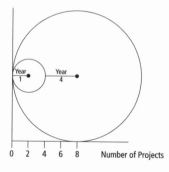

A. "The Decline of Benchmarking"

B. "The Explosive Growth of Benchmarking"

C. Underlying Data

	Number of Projects
Year One	2
Year Two	4
Year Three	6
Year Four	8

Figure 7. **The benchmarking outlook**

area-painting play a major role in subtle passing of information. The same creativity and discipline translate over to communicating results. The data on the white board are now designed locally to quickly convey the main message. Color and "control limits" show when a mere tendency becomes an actionable trend. Graphs replace tables of numbers. Multiple lines may show alternative future prospects instead of stopping at the current actual.

Call centers of many service industries have "tote boards" that show number of stations "up," number of stations in current use and longest customer wait time, so supervisors can make realtime decisions about staffing.

Great crimes of interpretation have been created in striving for simplicity of graphical display. Figure 7 shows two presentation charts that mislead. The first one suggests that benchmarking may be a passing fad, and the second suggests that benchmarking is growing "explosively." Actually, they both present the same underlying data. It all depends on what you are looking for.

The best discussion of graphical display appears in the works of Edward Tufte.[15] Here are some of the graphical sins that show up occasionally:

- presenting a partial period's data in comparison with a whole period's data

- presenting forecast data in a time series with actuals without labelling it as such

- interchanging trend and level data (In general, trend data is of more interest in mature and slower-moving concepts. Level data matters more to new and fast-moving issues. Either way, label which it is.)

- failing to use a semi-log scale in fast-moving trend data

- not labelling what any scale means

- print too small to read, in order to cram more information on a sheet of paper

- color-coding an original report, and then passing out black-and-white copies for interpretation

- not using round numbers as scale dividers (You can visually interpolate a number between 10 and 15 better than one between 10.9 and 14.2.)

- too much or too little rounding-off of numbers before using them in a graph or chart

- inconsistent (or dishonest) choice of "base" data

Baseline

The last point above, choice of base data, needs more attention. The general intention is easy to describe: What is normal? You always want to compare current results and future forecasts with "normal." But great arguments have occurred in determining what is normal.

Start with recent history. If nothing major has changed, the results from last month, last quarter or last year are candidates for "base." If you see large month-to-month variability, the previous year's monthly average might smooth out the variation. If you find seasonal variation, perhaps comparison with the same quarter or month in the previous year is appropriate. If you have a relevant long-cycle, you may need to use several years' data. Some political trends may only be analyzed well on a four-year cycle. Stock market data often is compared with previous highs or lows regardless of when they occurred. Heating oil usage has to take into account the weather, so the main concept is degree-days. How much oil was burned the last time it reached –10 degrees?

Sometimes a historical normal is adjusted to reflect a historical improvement trend. If the long-range improvement rate in some process (without unusual intervention) is one percent per year, and last year's level was 100, the base for this year might be set at 101. Anything over 101 for this year might then be interpreted as attributable to the planned intervention.

Another type of adjustment deals with breakthroughs. On October 1 of last year the performance in question jumped from the normal level of 60 per minute to 80 per minute. The base for this year should probably be 80, not 65 (the average of three quarters at 60 and one quarter at 80), unless the breakthrough only applies to fourth quarters.

The biggest challenge of all is when you have no historical data or experience. A new process has to live with a guesswork base until some data is generated, unless by benchmarking you can "borrow" experience from another organization that already has the process.

Objectives Matrix

Traditionally, if an organizational unit or group has several important measures, each measure receives a separate chart in a presentation and/or a separate page in a book and each is analyzed separately. In addition to plotting improvement trends, a marginal note and/or a "limit line" on a graph may represent a goal or target. For example, if you have six measures, and four are up and two are down, the general feeling is one of vague pleasure. If two are up and four are down it is vague discontent. There is no single "bottom line" statement of progress in either case.

But there is a better way! The Objectives Matrix form of display and analysis presents both trend and goal reference for all measures on the same chart and allows transparent combination of the measures by predetermined weighting to provide a single index value for the organization.[16]

Figure 8 shows an example of a completed Objectives Matrix. The loading sequence for an empty matrix is as follows:

1. Insert the Family of Measures "members" as column heads. Five or six measures is most common.

2. Provide an appropriate weighting of the measures in the row "Weight." (This is a very important step and requires participation of the local leader, since it in effect sets the group's direction.) The weights should add up to 100,

Mix Coverage	Discovery Reports	Development Index	Publications	Fragonator Use	Cross-Science		
42	17	105	1.0	56	26		**Performance**
70	25	150	5.0	90	40		**10**
65	23	145	4.5	86	37		**9**
60	21	140	4.0	82	34		**8**
55	19	135	3.5	78	31		**7**
50	17	130	3.0	74	28		**6**
45	15	120	2.5	70	24		**5** **Scores**
40	13	110	2.0	66	20		**4**
35	11	100	1.5	62	15		**3**
30	9	90	1.0	58	10		**2**
25	7	80	0.5	54	5		**1**
20	5	70	0	50	0		**0**
4.4	6.0	3.5	2.0	1.5	5.5		**Score**
30	20	20	10	10	10		**Weight**
132	120	70	20	15	55		**Value**

Objectives Matrix

Index
412

Figure 8.   Example of an objectives matrix

with no one element being more than 35 or less than 10.

3. Insert an appropriately "normal" base in row three for each measure.

4. Insert an agreed goal for each measure in row ten. The respective goals should have a consistent amount of "strive" factor (level of effort required to reach).

5. Fill in intermediate goal steps in rows four through nine and zero through two. The progressions can be arithmetically linear, geometrically linear, or even curvilinear (reflecting the common situation that the going gets tougher as you get closer to perfection).

6. After an amount of time passes (month, quarter, year), remeasure each family member and enter the new value in the "Performance" row.

7. For each measure, locate where the actual falls on the scale, determine the number of points (row value units) earned, and enter that value in the "Score" row.

8. Multiply Score by Weight in each column and enter the result in the "Value" row. Add the Value row numbers and enter the sum in Index. An index value of 300 means "no net progress." An index value of 1000 means attaining or exceeding all goals (and it is time to construct a new matrix). An index value of 412 simply

means a gain of 112 points since starting time. The percentage improvement (37 percent) is not especially meaningful.

You can use the matrix itself as a data-display unit by coloring in each column from the actual value down (or up) to the base value (three). Now you have a clear indicator of ups and downs that everyone in the work group can understand, even if the details of loading the matrix are not always clear. It also shows how far away the ultimate goals (10) are and how fast the organization is progressing toward each of the goals. It also provides a single index number statement of current level of performance that is a neutral-dimensioned bottom line.

XI.

REWARD AND RECOGNITION

CAREFUL OBSERVERS OF ORGANIZATIONS often comment that the true intentions of any organization are best detected in who is promoted and where the rewards and recognition systems devote the most attention. If promotions and bonuses seem to go to those behind long-term successes, employees (who are also careful observers) will emulate this behavior by getting into and working hard on long-term priorities. If, on the other hand, promotions and bonuses seem to go to "today's hero" based on short-term results, that's where employees will work hardest and "alignment with the strategic plan" becomes an empty term.

It is better for the organization to have one set of books. If what shows up in the mainstream measurement system also appears to be the basis for recognition and reward, focus is obtained and success is much more likely. Organizations with profit-sharing systems, for example, expect to get a focus on profits, even if most employees have difficulty seeing how what they do is related to profit. If the profit-sharing system is based on only the current year's profit, the short-term bias shows up again. A multi-year moving-average basis for profit sharing moves people to the longer range, but creates a complexity that only a few understand.

We have emphasized the long-range importance of a family of mostly physical variables being the "driver" of key financial variables. Believers in that concept should be driven towards the use of gain-sharing plans.[17] These plans reward employees if a set of predetermined variables improves more than "normal" in the course of a set time period, usually a year at a time.

The family of measures used to manage the business at the top of the full organization or the relevant location commonly becomes the basis for calculating the gain-sharing payouts. If the main signal for managing the business is "balanced improvement in productivity, quality and customer satisfaction," then the gain-sharing plan should be constructed from those same three variables. A huge advantage is that employees at the local level usually understand and identify with the details of cost saving, quality control and customer orientation better than a global profit calculation.

At the individual level, it also matters that individual recognition be given for reasons consistent with the organization's long-term improvement intentions. Employee-of-the-month programs in which only top management selects the recipients create the impression that employees should cozy up to top management. A system of on-the-spot recognition that one leader uses frequently and another uses rarely conveys a message about where

one should try to be transferred. Recognition that emphasizes heroic action to help the external customer more than
heroic action for internal improvement will shift attention
to customer-oriented processes.

XII.

TESTING
EXISTING MEASURES

I N THE REAL WORLD, an organization can rarely
create a completely new measurement system based
on this or any other set of guidelines. Often a company must improve its measurement system piecemeal,
where a perceived failure of the old system creates an
opening for improvement. Thus, would-be measurement
system improvers must possess the ability to criticize existing systems fairly. You might use these "test questions" to
appraise an existing set of measures and perhaps create an
opening wedge for further, more systematic improvement.

• Are we leaving out something very important? Are
  we including something not very important at this
  level?

• Are these measures well aligned with the measures
  of other groups

  . . . that we report to?

  . . . doing our type of work?

          . . . reporting to us?

          . . . upstream from us (internal suppliers)?

          . . . downstream from us (internal customers)?

- Do our employees seem to understand the measures and how to improve them? Do they have necessary training, tools and authority to work on improvement?

- Can we gather the underlying data for these measures economically and unobtrusively? Can we change the measures as needed?

- Do we try to cover a concept with a single surrogate measure when a multi-element index might be more meaningful (or vice versa)?

- Are our recognition and reward patterns consistent with what we are measuring (both executive and regular employees)?

- Are the measured results reported clearly enough, often enough and with only minor lag time? Can everyone explain them?

PART IV

SUMMARY
AND CONCLUSION

XIII.

SUMMARY AND CONCLUSION

T HE MAIN LESSONS PRESENTED in this book are the six points listed below. They apply to every organization with which the author has worked, regardless of size, industry or geography.

1. Measures should have their origins in customer needs as filtered through an organization's strategic plan.

2. The purpose of measures is to provide clear feedback to the organization's improvers at all levels.

3. A balanced family of measures is essential, for nothing is understood with just one measure.

4. The top of the organization and each division and department requires separate, but strategically related, families of measures for every cross-cutting process and work group.

5. Supplement measures of performance trends that identify continuous improvement results with benchmarked level measures so that you can establish realistic goals leading to break-through improvement projects where needed.

6. Not-for-profit organizations need to add long-range policy outcome indicators to their measurement systems to supplement and give direction to operationally oriented families of measures.

REFERENCES

1. *Random House Webster's College Dictionary.* New York: Random House, 1991.

2. Kaplan, Robert S. and David P. Norton. "The Balanced Scorecard: Measures That Drive Performance," *Harvard Business Review,* January–February, 1992 and "Putting the Balanced Scorecard to Work," *Harvard Business Review,* September–October, 1993.

3. Thor, Carl G. *The Measures of Success.* New York: Wiley, 1994.

4. Riggs, James L. and Glenn H. Felix. *Productivity by Objectives.* Englewood Cliffs, N.J.: Prentice-Hall, 1983.

5. Robinson, Alan G. "Simultaneous Improvements in Cost, Quality, Delivery and Flexibility," *Handbook for Productivity Measurement and Improvement,* edited by W. F. Christopher and Carl G. Thor. Portland, Oregon: Productivity Press, 1993, pp. 3–4.2.

6. Jenson, Richard L., James W. Brackner, and Clifford R. Skousen. *Management Accounting in Support of Manufacturing Excellence.* Montvale, N.J.: IMA Foundation for Applied Research, 1996.

7. Nonaka, Ikujiro and Hirotaka Takeuchi. *The Knowledge-Creating Company: How Japanese Companies Create the Dynamics of Innovation.* New York: Oxford University Press, 1995.

8. Collins, James C. and Jerry I. Porras. *Built to Last.* New York: Harper Business, 1994.

9. Conway, David L. "Common Staffing System" in Robert N. Lehrer, *White Collar Productivity.* New York: McGraw-Hill, 1983.

10. Thor, Carl G. "Measuring Environmental Results," Proceedings of Ninth World Productivity Congress, 1995. (Available from author.)

11. Akao, Yoji. *Quality Function Deployment.* Portland, Oregon: Productivity Press, 1995.

12. There is a section on predictive measures in "Advanced Systems of Corporate Performance Measurement," American Productivity & Quality Center, late 1997.

13. See note 12.

14. "Shingo Prize for Excellence in Manufacturing," Utah State University, 1996–97 Application Guidelines.

15. Tufte, Edward R. *The Visual Display of Quantitative Information.* Cheshire, Connecticut: Graphics Press, 1983.

16. See note 4.

17. See note 3.

FURTHER READING

Christopher, William F. and Carl G. Thor, eds. *Handbook for Productivity Measurement and Improvement*. Portland, Oregon: Productivity Press, 1993.

Kaplan, Robert S. and David P. Norton. "The Balanced Scorecard: Measures That Drive Performance," *Harvard Business Review,* January–February, 1992 and "Putting the Balanced Scorecard to Work," *Harvard Business Review,* September–October, 1993.

Sink, Scott and Thomas Tuttle. *Planning and Measurement in Your Organization of the Future*. Atlanta: IIE Press, 1989.

Thor, Carl G. *The Measures of Success*. New York: Wiley, 1994.

ABOUT THE AUTHOR

Carl G. Thor is President of JarrettThor International, a
consulting firm specializing in performance measurement
and related issues. Previously he was President and Vice
Chairman of the American Productivity & Quality Center
and before that he was employed in the food and petro-
leum industries in the United States and Brazil.

Thor is also affiliated with the World Confederation
of Productivity Science, the International Service Quality
Association, and the Shingo Prize for Manufacturing
Excellence. He is the author of six books and hundreds
of articles and a frequent speaker on productivity and
quality issues.

771 Battery Place
Alexandria, VA 22314
Phone: (703) 548-7306
Fax: (703) 548-7908
E-mail: jarretthor@aol.com